NINO GUGUNISHVILI

There Was a Garden Once

Copyright © 2025 by Nino Gugunishvili

All rights reserved. No part of this publication may be reproduced, stored or transmitted in any form or by any means, electronic, mechanical, photocopying, recording, scanning, or otherwise without written permission from the publisher. It is illegal to copy this book, post it to a website, or distribute it by any other means without permission.

First edition

This book was professionally typeset on Reedsy. Find out more at reedsy.com

To Maia

Contents

1. HELLO, NICE TO MEET YOU! — 1
2. LATE BLOOMERS — 4
3. THAT SCARY FIFTY — 12
4. AN ODE TO BIRKENSTOCKS — 15
5. A TALE OF A RED LIPSTICK — 18
6. ON GRIEF — 21
7. PASTA OF OUR CHILDHOOD — 25
8. IDIOT — 29
9. SEVERAL REASONS WHY IT'S GOOD TO BE A WRITER — 32
10. OUR WARS — 34
11. WINTER. LOVE. LOSS. — 37
12. ARE WE THE CHAMPIONS? — 39
13. THIRTY-EIGHT DAYS — 42
14. MY NEIGHBOR BENJAMIN — 44
15. THE POOL — 46
16. ALMOST DUST — 49
17. I WANT TO… — 51
18. WHITE JEANS — 55
19. LITTLE BLACK LAPTOP — 57
20. STILL ME? — 59
21. THERE WAS A GARDEN ONCE — 61
22. INSTEAD OF A PROLOGUE & AN EPILOGUE — 66
23. YOU KNOW NOTHING — 69

24 HOW TO END A BOOK? 71
About the Author 75

1

HELLO, NICE TO MEET YOU!

"Let me introduce myself." How silly that phrase sounds. How can I introduce myself to someone who doesn't know me at all? What should I say? That I'm a film critic turned writer, now writing in a language that isn't my native one? Let's get to the name, and that's where the messy part begins. Before I even say my first and last names, dear reader, chances are you're gone. My name is Nino.

Don't get me wrong, I'm pretty happy with the name my parents chose when I was born. There was no other option but to call me Nino in honor of my grandmother.

When you pronounce my first and last names, it's not easy. Nino Gugunishvili. It's long. Try spelling it to someone over the phone when making an appointment or a booking. That's hell!

The thing is, Gugunishvili is not precisely my last name. In Georgian, it's spelled with ღ, not გ (which is the equivalent of the English G), and ღ sounds closest to Gh or the famous R in French. But in French, I'd have to become Gougounichvili – so, basically, it's too complicated, and easy to misspell. "Dear Mr.

Gugunish," one of the emails I received many years ago said. I've kept it in my collection of funny misuses of my last name. While it sounds odd, it also highlights how little we understand each other's cultures through names and surnames.

On the bright side, you can reinvent and rediscover yourself. You can imagine, dream, transform, change, or try on different identities.

When I wrote my debut novel and was preparing for publication, I considered choosing a pen name. "Gugunishvili" is too long and too difficult to remember," I've been told countless times, but I decided to stick with it. In a way, it already was a change of identity. Paradoxically, diving into another language felt like assimilating into the foreign terrain and finding your new self.

It's probably one of the most mysterious things about writing, choosing the language in which you're writing your book, when your mind, your vocabulary, and your phrasing switch instantly, and often you start remembering words that were stored somewhere far, far away in your memory until that very moment when you sit down and write. It's as if you're living in several multi-lingual, different, and often opposite worlds, each with its realities, and you're able to explore them only if you use another language; that's when those imaginative doors or passages open, letting you in, a little like Alice in Wonderland. It's like being an actor, diving into another person's life and living it as your own for a given moment, transforming into something new, unknown, and unexpected.

The second part of the introduction is even messier when it comes to positioning myself as an author. Am I a successful author? A well-known writer? And the answer is simple; well, dearest reader, it appears there's a long road ahead. Very, very,

very, long road ahead. Just an hour ago, I boosted a post on Instagram, in the hope that the fact of my tiny, precious book being discounted would reach every non-fiction, memoir lover, and Kindle owner on planet Earth. It's an illusion, I know. But isn't it the sweetest?

Convincing someone to read your book sometimes feels like walking through the desert of sand. Does it sound too cliché? Shall I say that the book is funny? Shall I say it'll make them laugh? But what if they don't want to laugh? What if they woke up in a grim mood? What if I say it's honest? But who needs that honesty? And the fact that it's autobiographical doesn't add any more interest to it, I suppose. My autobiography is not like Einstein's. I don't have any scientific discoveries that would definitely serve humanity. What I have are my thoughts and observations, along with some stories about my family and friends, and life. Mind you, some friends don't even know I'm writing about them. (Yet).

So, who will read this book? Maybe a random someone just like me, posing too many idiotic questions, someone who enjoys solitude, someone who loves chocolate, someone whose name is…

2

LATE BLOOMERS

I started writing letters to you when you were in the hospital. Two years ago. I didn't know how to cope with so much worry, anger, sadness, angst, pain, and all I could think of was writing, in the hope that you'd read them someday. Someday – never came. What came was (is) a life without you. Strange, empty, and so unimaginably different.

Two days ago, I went to my father's cemetery. I've been there so many times, in all seasons. I love the place; secluded. It was a warm, beautiful, sunny November day. I know it's not the best idea to start a story with the weather, but it really was a perfect autumn day. "A perfect jacket weather," as you'd say.

My paternal grandmother and my great-grandmother are buried there, too. It's not far from your grave, but I didn't want to visit yours. My feet hurried out, and in a minute, I was already walking on the avenue. The contrast between the calm of the cemetery and the central avenue was so daunting that, for a second, I held my breath. It was as if the sound had been muted, and then it came back blasting with the highest volume.

I ran, realizing again and again and again that you are gone. I ran into the noisy street, leaving the cemetery behind.

Suppose I could rip the calendar pages off and get back to our lives before mid-November 2023. You would have called me and asked about my plans for the day, and I would have told you that it was my father's day and that I would later visit a newly opened Italian café. You'd be content, saying we'd have to pop in there too, and in several days we would, and you would have a steak, medium rare, and I would have a carbonara, you would have joked that I'm always ordering a pasta, and we would laugh, but you're right, I love a good pasta, and I hate the "would." My mind switches and mixes past and present tenses. The reality with you and without you morphs into one another, and so is my life; with you, without you.

This book begins with pieces I wrote while you were still here and follows the two years I've lived since you left. I'm struggling to finish it. I don't want to finish it. I like this monologue, a dialogue that never ends, never stops.

I couldn't imagine writing and publishing a book that you hadn't had a chance to read. That you haven't been happy about, the journey you haven't been an integral part of, from the beginning to the end. I can't get rid of the feeling that something is always missing, and that's you. Your voice on my phone, checking in about the progress, about the cover, about the editing process, about the blurb. "Hello, writer, how's it going?" You'd call me. "Hello, writer," I'd reply, and vent, that I'm stuck, that I'm lazy, that I have no idea why I started writing, and what'll come out of it. You'd listen and come over for a coffee, and we would talk as if we had never talked before, squeezing in important and not-so-important news from our lives into those coffee breaks.

My debut novel featured your favorite phrase: "Friday

Evening, Eight O'clock," the time you usually suggested for our Friday gatherings and evenings out. "After Eight," to be precise. I borrowed it from you. That was a different life, a life apart. And now? Now I'm thinking about the title, but in vain. I've lost my favorite reader.

For the thousandth time, I watched You've Got Mail yesterday. Whenever we were in New York, we would visit Café Lalo, where the characters of Meg Ryan and Tom Hanks meet in the movie. I wanted to see the Apthorp building, where Nora Ephron once lived, but we never got the chance. On one of our trips, we visited Carrie Bradshaw's apartment.

We were busy and touristy. We were happy. I remember, during one of our last trips, as we exited Central Park, you told me how you wanted to end your next book. "It'll be a happy end, despite all her mishaps, don't worry, she'll be okay," you told me, referring to the main character. Or did you tell me you just came up with a premise of the book? Weird thing about memory is that it rearranges events, and I can't precisely remember what you told me that day. I know it was important, but I'm unable to double-check it with you. I remember the tiredness from walking. "We need coffee!" you probably added, and I guess we went to the Le Pain Quotidien and probably had a carrot cake or a goat cheese salad.

When writing, we were each other's Google. A movie quote, a poem, a phrase, a word, or an old song - we double-checked everything with one another. For a second, I can't remember what Turkish pretzels are called, and I want to dial your number to ask you about our trips to Istanbul, our walks, and buying them just before lunch or dinner. Walking, laughing, taking quick bites, savoring the baklavas, stopping to buy pashminas, because it was cold, and you forgot all your jackets back home.

You made us fall in love with Istanbul; it was always our top destination. "No one understands your English here," you teased me when I shouted in the taxi, the driver taking a U-turn opposite the traffic. Unlike me, you never had a problem entering into a chat with taxi drivers and shopping assistants and always got what you asked for: directions, dishes, and a wine list.

More than these trips, I miss the ordinary days—the days we often ignore, the "passing days," the uneventful ones.

So much of our shared memories come from the trips we've taken in the last 10 years - the short weekend ones, the birthday ones, the longer US ones. But the best part was returning home. "I'm home, of course I'm home," the main character says in your book as it ends.

I rarely look at your old messages, but I'm sure there are numerous with just one line – "Are you home? I'm coming over", or another one inviting me over to your place.

"I'm home, come over".

So, I want to think you're in the midst of your travel somewhere and haven't yet come home.

I knew I had to get out of bed and write about you. It's 6:30 am now.

Claudia Cardinale passed away yesterday. Robert Redford on September 16th. Their beautiful pictures and tributes are everywhere. I loved this one for Claudia Cardinale from the Cannes Film Festival:

"The girl with a suitcase journeyed across the world. Through

Europe, Hollywood, South America, Canada, Australia, Russia.... She laughed, sang, danced, loved, and shone before the cameras of the greatest... An adventurous, free-spirited, and fiery Italian, she captured our hearts in film after film- nearly 150 – always with a luminous grace of joy and boldness...."

The first thing I instinctively wanted to do after hearing about Redford's passing was call you to share the news. Then I remembered that Out of Africa was one of your favorite movies, and we both frequently quoted the "I had a farm in Africa" opening line.

I'm looking at photos of Robert Redford, Claudia Cardinale, and Alain Delon on Instagram, and I keep thinking of you, remembering you, and mourning you. It makes me recall our love, admiration, and obsession with cinema. It's because of Butch Cassidy and the Sundance Kid. Because of Alain Delon and Claudia Cardinale in Visconti's The Leopard, and because of Romy Schneider and Alain Delon's love story, those films became part of us, shaping us —our imagination, tastes, dreams, the way we talked, the way we dressed, and how we chose our careers and jobs.

Whenever someone said that reading our books felt like watching a movie, we were happy.

"Don't you think that Cat on a Hot Tin Roof has one of the greatest endings?" You would often inquire. There was nothing to argue about. You were right. There will never be another Paul Newman and Elizabeth Taylor duo.

'Some things definitely take more time than we expected.' You'd say, referring to starting to write later in life.

"Yep, we are late bloomers. Both you and me." I would nod as we drank coffee on my balcony.

One of the last times I saw you, you held the glossy cover of your upcoming book. A contagious, glowing happiness, yours, mine. A beautiful pink cover with a butterfly on it. "A little south of Eden," the title says.

Life interrupted.

I had a farm in Africa.

We were the late bloomers. That's precisely the way we were.

I don't remember when you gave me this pearl bracelet. Maybe on one of my birthdays? It's so tight on my wrist that I can't take it off, unless I open a tiny lock, which is too fragile even to touch, and I'm afraid to break it accidentally. I don't want to open it. I like the contrast of white pearls on my tanned wrist. The tan will dissolve in a few weeks, but today the contrast is lovely. I don't want to take it off; on the contrary, I want to wear everything you ever gifted to me, another bracelet, a ring, a brooch of a fat seal with green and yellow little stones on its head. I think you bought it some twenty years ago, and I never wore it. In fact, I had forgotten about it and found it the other day, in one of the jewelry boxes in my drawer.

I sense you almost physically. I'm not letting you go. Tiny pearls on my wrist hold us together: our memories, our laughs, our anguish, our setbacks, our dreams. We're connected. Making gifts brought you immense happiness, with the immediacy of seeing the recipient's reaction, the joy of gifting someone, and the thoughtfulness of choosing what to give—the rush of bringing it over.

Those green leather flats we bought in NY, on our way to the Marc Jacobs bookstore, with the intention of getting you a lucky keychain, and you asked me to try them on, pretending you wanted them for your mom. Later, you almost threw them at me when we returned home from that trip. We never made it to the bookstore, and I didn't buy you the gift I had promised.

"You are the worst shopper", you've told me many times, and it's more than true.

We've been friends for a long time — long before our NY journey — but it seems to me that we rediscovered ourselves in our friendship during our first visit to New York. The mature, elder, conscious, trusting, treasuring each other's friendship, of stepping into a different experience, dealing with something bigger side by side. A story for the two of us, one that we never tired of retelling to a broader circle of friends.

The intense fight we had when you bought me a vest, and how we laughed afterward at my foolish reaction, my inability to appreciate, and my quick temper. I would give everything to go on more trips with you. To have more gifts from you. More conversations with you. I would give every day of my life to spend one more day with you.

Since you left, I've been thinking about:
Sadness.
Boredom.
Guilt.

I have zero coping with you not being here. It's a hamster wheel/Groundhog Day. By the way, it was never our movie.

I think that, almost two years after you left, our tastes might have changed. I realized it yesterday, when I bought a fancy jacket embroidered with minuscule crystals. I wanted you to see it. I know you would have liked it, as it's so different from what I usually wear –the jeans and sneakers. Much more age-appropriate, as you'd say, plus it's from one of the brands you loved.

LATE BLOOMERS

I'm typing, and tiny white pearls of my bracelet are clicking on the keyboard rhythmically, circling my right wrist, circling and locking our lives, tighter. Your son is getting married, and I have to buy him a wedding present. Any ideas?

3

THAT SCARY FIFTY

Whenever I want to say how old I am, I block out the numbers, not because I want to lie, but because I'm struggling to remember the exact number. 45? 46? 47? 48? Then I calculate it on my phone, or if I'm too lazy to figure it out, I call my close friend, who is the same age as me, and ask her. She's probably already fed up with me asking the same question repeatedly, but she always responds with the exact number, and we laugh at my inability to remember my age.

Several days ago, I thought I was getting fifty this summer, which was shocking. Fifty? Fifty? No. It can't be true. I can't be getting fifty, I protested. My mind refused to take in that information. Fifty is not how I feel. In a society that implies you should sum up your life by a certain age, look back, and pat yourself on the shoulder for your achievements, I'm not even close to that goal. I'm in the beginning. I'm a late bloomer. I still have time before getting fifty, and honestly, if you ask me, I'd say I'm thirty. I feel like thirty. I want to be thirty and not forty-eight. I still have many things ahead. Mind-blowing love affairs, luxurious travels, and new books written. I need a small house in the woods and dogs. Maybe a cat, too. I want a round and massive old table in the living room of my future writing escape.

I like that house to be decorated in the best hygge, Scandinavian, cozy aesthetic to justify the thousands of hours spent on Instagram and Pinterest. I want to go to Lapland and try dog sledding. I want to travel to Vienna and buy Christmas decorations at the Christmas market.

Aren't these dreams a little naïve and immature? How can I be getting close to fifty? I still have silly things to do!

Does it mean I deny getting older? I have never considered age to be something one must hide. But too often during social gatherings now, I can't get rid of the feeling that I'm much older than anyone in the room, and quite honestly, I feel like an old crow. Okay, maybe I'm exaggerating, but I feel I'm from a different era; I talk differently and dress differently, not to mention my tastes in movies and music. I feel very retro or out of place, especially if I'm wearing my black velvet jacket, which I quite like and is probably the only "sophisticated" outfit in my entire wardrobe. Additionally, it pairs well with almost anything, such as jeans or black pants.

Today, my cousin told me she didn't want to go to a place she was invited to because she didn't want to feel like an "old aunt" among people considerably younger than us, and I mentally agreed. It was precisely how I felt. We don't want to play young; heavy hangovers and all-night dancing are not ours anymore, mine, at least for sure. After a glass of red wine, I get a headache the next day. I can't stand loud music, and generally, I'm socially awkward. After almost two years of sweatpants and pajamas, it's challenging to return to formal attire, let alone survive the small talk with strangers over a glass of your preferred beverage. I'd want to be tall, thin, and blonde, but I'm not. Instead, I'm, let's say, slightly overweight, my hair is colored "brunette," and right now, as I'm writing this, I'm wearing an "I love New York" gray hoodie, which is my go-to workout outfit.

I'll tell you what I'm secretly dreaming of. I dream of fitting into non-existent skinny white jeans. I want to have an immaculate pedicure. There's something unachievable and dreamy in "immaculate". Also, I dream of thick, blonde, highlighted, wavy hair and tanned, toned arms. "Hello, it's me…" – Do you hear me singing that popular Adele song? Right. I wonder if the world population will know the songs of the first half of the 21st century in two hundred years?

In two hundred years, perhaps Google will still be there, so the younger generation can always Google, but before that, I'm going to drink my black coffee that'll wash all the remaining calcium from my bones, from a mug my cousin, the one who doesn't want to feel like an "old aunt," gifted me many years ago and I'm going to check, what's she's going to wear, to knock the youngsters off, while she transforms into a dancing queen for the night. "You are a dancing queen, young and sweet, only seventeen… yeah, yeah," Remember ABBA? Oh, for god's sake, go, Google!

4

AN ODE TO BIRKENSTOCKS

B lame it on age, blame it on my recent obsession with safety and comfort, Birkenstocks and Puffer coats will be a part of my favorite things from now on, and forever. If I'm not cremated, I'll ask to put my last pair of Birkenstocks and my last puffer coat into my coffin. I'll be fine wearing them even if I'm dead.

If you have recently vowed never to rebuy high heels and prefer comfortable shoes—be it sneakers, flip-flops, or sandals— nice to meet you!

I assume we have had similar experiences with shoes and the discomfort they can cause. I suggest that at different stages of our lives, we have fallen for brands that lure us into the gloss and glamour of beautiful, must-have shoes we feel compelled to buy. But if you have ever trotted the streets of Sorrento, Istanbul, Boston, or Tbilisi on high heels (trot may not be the exact word here), you probably know what I mean. I can feel everything you have felt. I have struggled and tortured my feet, too. I see you. I am you. I was you until I fell in love with

Birkenstocks, and my life changed. I am obsessed with them and want them in as many colors as possible. Red, of course, darker red, sure! Black? – No question! And now I'm buying the khaki ones too. I hope you don't judge me, and even if you do, I don't care. I wholeheartedly hated my feet for half of my life. However, as in every relationship, we've had our ups and downs, love-hate moments, and reconciliations.

Among the many fashion revolutions, big and small, like Yves Saint Laurent's famous "Le Smoking" or Chanel's little black dress, Birkenstocks are no less iconic. In all their casualness, they highlight the socio-cultural factor, simplicity, and comfort we tend to choose over mega-expensive footwear, no matter the occasion. Whether we stay home or go out, we can wear Birkenstocks.

"Beauty needs sacrifice," – a saying we've heard far too often when we were young, doesn't work anymore.

If shoes can give you a sense of community, Birkenstock does that. You can see everyone wearing Birkenstocks everywhere. At the airports, in the streets, in the cafes and museums, in shops, in the parks, in the offices, at the beach, so many feet. So many liberated feet and happy faces.

Another new must-have, let's not forget, is a puffer coat. Everywhere you go, wherever you are, you see an army of puffer coats of different brands and sizes floating in the streets of cities across the globe.

I'm sure you have it in your wardrobe. As my friend once stated, it's not just a coat or an item of clothing; it's an investment, and I agree. It's almost a global uniform. Puffer coats symbolize a unified style chosen by people seeking warmth, stability, and comfort. Puffer coats quickly become as iconic as Jeans or leggings, transcending age, class, race, and nationality.

What about wearing a light puffer coat and Birkenstocks together? I have to try. I will let you know.

5

A TALE OF A RED LIPSTICK

Contrary to me, my mom is loyal to one brand. Dior. I have never witnessed such devotion, determination, and zest with which she's searching for her favorite lipstick, even though she knows that the answer from the beauty consultants at the shops locally or internationally will almost always be – "Oh, sorry, we don't have it anymore. It's a limited edition." However, my mom doesn't want a similar color from a different Dior collection, even if it's the brand-new one that just arrived in stores. She doesn't care.

"Dior's Diorific lipstick comes out only once or twice a year, sometimes on Christmas," a lovely woman at the Vienna airport told me as she watched me desperately searching the Dior cosmetics stands. Other shades and textures were also available. Diorific 005 was, of course, missing. We've been chasing it all around international airports and the cities we've traveled to, but in vain. That Diorific red lipstick in a shiny golden tube is hiding from us, no matter how hard we try to find it. There are thousands of others out there, new ones, glossier, shinier, with a more extensive palette, but we need that tiny golden tube number 005 because that particular lipstick is a history, a memory, confidence, a hope, in a world out of control, it symbolizes the stability of owning one thing that you grew attached to over the years. You don't want to change; the one thing that defines you, shows your personality, tells your story, makes you—you. It's an endless love in a tiny tube. One little attribute you're not ready to part with is the color —the soft shade and its vibrancy. You want to have it with you at all times, regardless of your mood, season, or age.

Maybe I should write a letter to Dior, telling them how enamored my mother is with that particular edition of red lipstick. I would write, Dear Dior, I'm writing you on behalf of my mother, who's a lifelong fan of yours. She's been your loyal customer for ages, for almost forty or fifty years, from the time the Dior brand appeared in the Soviet Union, precisely, Moscow, and I remember how every time we traveled there, the first thing we did was go to the corner shop of our hotel and buy two things. Dior lipstick and a Lancôme blush, standing in the long crowds in winter. At that time, as you may understand, dear Dior, it was our glimpse into the world of fulfilled dreams.
   It gave us the feeling that we, too, belonged to the thousands of beautiful, badass women from Paris to Rome and from Rome to New York, whom we so wanted to resemble, with whom we had something in common, and who shared the same love for the iconic red lipstick. My mom was no exception. She deserved it, and she deserves it even more now. Not that she ever lacked confidence, but it made her shine even brighter. So, please, dear Dior, bring that lipstick back in stock to make her happy because, yes, lipstick = confidence. Lipstick = motivation.

Lipstick is a manifesto about feeling young, being young, and looking forward to magic.

6

ON GRIEF

I don't know how to write about grief and sorrow. I don't know if the words will ever express the emptiness, numbness, demotivation, or anger. I miss you. Everything changed. Our lives changed. "Life changes in the instant,"- Joan Didion wrote in "The Year of Magical Thinking".

I've flipped that book online many times, but I've never bought it. Maybe now it's the time, but I couldn't make myself read past the few opening lines. Just one phrase stuck with me. "Life changes in the instant". I don't know how to live and be without you, without calling you, chatting with you, traveling with you, laughing with you, gossiping with you, sharing the news of our lives, all the silly, tiny, unimportant details. I will never have anyone like you. So close, so dear, so mind-alike. I don't want to post pictures online. I want to stay silent. I so badly want to go back to any time before November 15. I even miss going to the hospital every day. Sometimes I feel like my heart will explode from sadness, but it doesn't. I can't cry. I'm waking up every day to the world without you. I'm alive and you are not. Sometimes I don't think about you for an hour in a row, and then it hits me that you're gone. I can't, I don't want to write those words. Gone.

Grief is playing on the phone all day.

Grief is laughing while watching a dumb movie.

Grief is frantically buying Santa Claus and Christmas tree decorations.

Grief is sleeping.

Grief is staying awake or waking up abruptly in the middle of the night.

Grief is not wanting to get out of bed.

Grief is not wanting to stay in bed.

Grief is the wish to run away somewhere far.

Grief is not wanting to leave the house.

Grief is a coffee capsule you left me.

Grief is your white umbrella; you forgot to take it home.

Grief is realizing that exactly one month ago, you were alive. As always at my place, we met in the evening and sat in the kitchen, and drank coffee.

Grief is replaying that last conversation in my mind.

Grief is knowing you won't be able to read any books I'll ever write. Grief is knowing you'll never be able to write a new book of your own. You haven't even finished your second one.

Grief is your empty house, your sad dog, and the empty chair at your kitchen table.

Grief is this Christmas without you.

Grief is the New Year without you.

Grief is Istanbul without you.

Grief is New York and Boston without you.

Grief is living after you. Without you.

Grief is pain.

Grief is the story I won't tell you ever again. The dirty jokes, the books we'd read and discuss.

Grief is the movies we'll never watch, and the new ones you'll never see.

Grief is sipping a glass of wine without you and laughing without you.

Grief is posting online and knowing you won't be the first to comment, send a heart, or a clapping hand emoji.

Grief is not being able to create new memories and only revisiting the dearest ones in my mind over and over again.

Grief is saying thank you for your friendship. You were always a better friend than I.

Grief is saying sorry.

Grief is feeling guilty.

Grief is hearing your voice out of nowhere—the nuances of every phrase you say, the intonation. Grief is seeing you vividly, wearing your dark blue jacket and white blouse somewhere in New York, deciding where to go next, and whether we're close enough to the place we've just booked for dinner.

Grief is anger.

Grief is rage.

Grief is a beautiful winter day you won't see.

Grief is life not stopping.

Grief is living in slow motion.
   Grief is thinking and remembering.
   Grief is not wanting to think about what happened.
   Grief is trying to forget.
   Grief is light, and grief is darkness.

Grief is being cheesy and sentimental and not giving the fuck about it.

Grief is seeing your phone number and wanting to call you every single day.

Grief is learning to live without you for the rest of my life.

7

PASTA OF OUR CHILDHOOD

I guess I fell in love with Italy that snowy winter day when my mom and I hurried to the post office in the tiny town of Zheleznitse to collect my very own Ciccio Bello doll, sent by a lovely Italian woman named Patricia from Italy to Czechoslovakia. I fantasized about that baby doll with a pacifier, wearing a blue dress. It cried and stopped when you hugged it. This was the first gift I received from somewhere far and unknown, with my name written all over the vast, dark-brown paper parcel. I was six. It was long before Amazon, the Internet, email, and Facebook. It was 1980. Yes, it was that long ago.

My first encounter with Italian cuisine and an Italian temperament also happened in Czechoslovakia that same year. Pizza, Lasagna, Spaghetti, Pasta —these are dishes that neither my brother nor my mother had any idea about, and they only saw in foreign magazines and movies.

As my feet were considerably weaker than those of the children my age, and I had trouble walking "normally," we had to spend three months in one of the children's rehabilitation centers, alongside Russians, French, Czechs, and Italians. Parents who couldn't leave their children for a lengthy period of treatment stayed there and, of course, needed to communicate with each other. In contrast, we, the children, went to various classes to improve our physical health. One of the Italian ladies I liked most was Luciana, a tall, dark-haired woman with a son named Giovanni. I think it was Luciana who brought the first homemade Pizza and later Lasagna for us to try.

"Gugunishvili, telephone," I can still hear that voice with a Czech or Italian accent, my mom rushing to answer the call from Tbilisi, thousands of miles away. In that little Czech town, three of us: my brother, mom, and I, had to learn to live in an international environment, a considerable part of which consisted of tasting different food and co-existing with people who were just like us, only spoke a foreign language, but when language barriers were insurmountable, food came in as a savior.

Fried sausages, rogalics, knedliki dumplings, spaghetti, pizza, lasagna, and pasta entered our lives one after another. In the evenings, tired Italian mothers would drink Cinzano and Martini, with my mom joining them sometimes.

I didn't like dining at home; I loved eating everything the Italian mommas made. Their menu had nothing in common with ours. My mom managed to communicate with Italians using a mixture of French, English, Russian, and Italian, yet she was never misunderstood.

"You probably won't get to Sicily, but my sister Gabriella lives in Rome. Keep her number and don't forget to call her if you happen to come to Rome," Luciana told my mom one day while we ate another round of delicious pasta she cooked in no time. At that moment, the idea of my mom traveling to Italy felt pretty unbelievable. Mom thanked her and tucked the small piece of paper with Gabriella's number into her pocket. Italy was too distant.

Two years later, my mother finally traveled to Rome and met Gabriella at a beautiful Italian restaurant, followed by a movie night to watch one of Liliana Cavani's masterpieces.

My mother kept correspondence with her Italian friends for years, until the letters started coming ripped open. "Other people" were reading them too. Those "other people" matter-of-factly told her before one of her trips to Italy that they knew she had friends there.

When she recounts those trips during soviet times, there's so much laughter, pleasure, and fun involved that I almost envy her. When I asked her why she stopped writing letters and sending greeting cards to Luciana and other women with whom she spent several months every year, side by side, she said she felt utterly offended that someone other than her friends would read them.

I still don't speak Italian, and my knowledge of Czech is now forgotten, but I vividly remember Luciana running down the corridor shouting: Cinquanta Cinque! Cinquanta Cinque! Cinquanta Cinque! and jumping off the scales. Her weight was perfect, and the many birthday celebrations for the children and parents didn't affect her flawless body. Auguri! We shouted when blowing out the birthday candles. I wonder if she's still alive and how her son Giovanni is doing. I often think about finding them somewhere in Sicily...

That first Ciccio Bello doll is now long lost, but I still have another one, which my father brought back from Italy years later. But nothing compares to the ecstasy of receiving the first one in a small post office, unwrapping the parcel hurriedly, that delight of receiving a gift, owning something I had wished for, and the excitement of the wish coming true, being fulfilled. For that alone — among the best childhood memories of my entire life — I'll be forever grateful to Italy.

8

IDIOT

She believes I'm not styling my hair correctly. She says I'm smoking too many cigarettes. She's worried I might be predisposed to osteoporosis because of my early menopause. She fears I'll have to rely on a monthly pension of about $90 when I'm older—if I don't write several bestsellers by then. She wants me to win a Pulitzer, Nobel, Booker, or any other major literary award. Next summer, I'll turn fifty. We agreed that fifty is the new thirty and seventy is the new fifty. Sometimes she calls me an idiot, and I agree with her. Considering that I have no official job and mostly stay at home—or, as one of my friends says, "lie at home"—and I depend financially on others, it's accurate. I'm a complete idiot, hidden behind the "writer." A struggling writer. A doubting writer. A not very confident writer. A procrastinator.

The Complete idiot phase of my life began several years ago when I decided that putting my incredible thoughts down on paper was much more exciting than planning monthly TV grids. Ambitiously, I started writing in a foreign language, with Paris and London as the primary settings for my future bestseller.

I thought I was already Françoise Sagan. I wrote every single day from winter to summer. By the end of summer, my novel was ready. It was published two years later, and my friends and immediate family members were all mind-blown. And?

And then, I read the first negative review. "Nice cover, wrong book," it said. "Too many errors," the second reader wrote, "It's all over the place," another wrote. "Nice, but too long…" After the thirteenth review, I had to choose between quitting writing altogether or continuing to read reviews. I decided to stop reading reviews. One thing was crystal clear: I was not Françoise Sagan. Two more jobs, and three more books later, I still wasn't, and the dreams of strolling at Côte d'Azur in white pants and sandals, leisurely sipping champagne, vanished. Not that anyone from a Nobel or Pulitzer Prize committee called me either.

La Dolce Vita – was someone else's, not mine. My mom's friend Helen suggested that I write shorter books. "No one reads long books anymore, darling," she stated, attempting to show me the shortest road to worldwide stardom. I wrote three short books: nonfiction essays and a novella.

The other day, I met my reader at the beauty salon, and she excitedly told me she loved my latest collection of essays. It appeared my mom gifted it to her. It felt strange. I wasn't ready to meet a fan in a hair salon, of all the places! The one thought I had on my mind while we were waiting for our turn to color our hair and trim our brows was *"Shit! Now she knows so many quite personal things about me!"*

I can't handle either criticism or praise. My hair now is sixty fucking shades darker. I'm not a brunette anymore.

You're free to read all of the books I wrote. You can even leave a bad review. Don't worry about me. I'll ask my mom to give me one-half of Xanax and read them, well, sometime in my next life. Or better, I'll have roasted chestnuts she made yesterday evening, and pretend I'm strolling through Paris, nonchalantly. *Bonjour, Tristesse?*

9

SEVERAL REASONS WHY IT'S GOOD TO BE A WRITER

You can always use writing as an excuse for skipping boring meetings, and don't listen to those who might tell you otherwise. Have they struggled to write an opening paragraph better than in War and Peace? Probably not. So, don't bother.

You can steal some very personal stories from your friends and shamelessly use them in your novel or your short story, without being forever banned from their lives. You're immortalizing them, so they should be thankful, and what if you receive a Pulitzer or a Nobel Prize? They will be proud. Maybe in a hundred years, but still. Time doesn't matter when it's about writing.

No one will think you're crazy, seeing you talking to yourself in public, because you can always say you're mastering your character's monologue.

If your boss catches you googling something utterly unrelated to your work, like the lifespan of a rabbit, you can always claim you're doing research for your next book and give him that look of a future best-selling author.

If you never really liked your name, you can change it to a pen name without embarrassing your family or forcing them to cut you out of the family forever.

You can jump at any opportunity to travel alone, saying you've just signed up for a writer's retreat.

You can watch Netflix all day because you're casting actors for their roles in your future best-seller.

You can hang up the phone on anyone without sounding rude because the specific line came to your mind at that moment, and you need to write it down immediately.

You can be the only living writer known to your loved ones, with whom they can hang around, drink a coffee, or anything more substantial, and they will pamper you.

Few things in life are better than hearing "My aunt is a writer," believe me.

10

OUR WARS

My friend brought me a perfect birthday gift—a set of Estée Lauder moisturizers. I'm eager to open them. I want to believe they will miraculously make my skin glowing and fresh, and then, I'll see a different me in the mirror, minus ten years or even fifteen. I follow the healthy lifestyle trend when it comes to exercise. I regularly do Pilates and Aqua Aerobics. Okay, I'm a heavy smoker and coffee addict, and I know it's shit for the bones, for skin, for hair, teeth, and everything else, but apart from that, I guess I may suggest being on the "healthy living" spectrum, but that's not what I'm wondering now. I'm wondering when the anti-aging war began. When did we start denying the natural aging process? I certainly missed that moment. I missed the moment we entered the stage of our lives when we battle everything. Our weight, our physical looks, our wrinkles, our bodies, our self-esteem, our beliefs, our social responsibilities, our political views, our memories, our relationships, and our personal history. We transform into battling forty-somethings, not liking ourselves or the world around us. We become angry and protective.

OUR WARS

The other day at the yoga studio, I gave my usual spot to another girl, and she lit up instantly. She seemed so genuinely happy and surprised. At first, I didn't understand why. What was so exciting about standing a little closer to the yoga instructor? It was a tiny gesture, something entirely unimportant, but suddenly, I realized what made her so happy and why she had an astonished look on her pretty face. At that moment, I told her she could take my space; she didn't have to fight. She had to switch off her constant fighting and defender mode and relax. For an entire hour during that particular day, she didn't have to protect what was hers, prove herself, and fight for her place. She could forget that, and she was grateful.

Think for a second how many things we have to fight for every single day, how many things grate on our nerves, how many skills we need not to be left out. Driving in traffic, planning the day, dropping children off at school, not being late to work/ hairdresser/ shopping/ doctor appointments/ pet groomers/ and the list goes on. Everyone needs to be on time, and everyone frets about it. We can't be weak. We must always be strong; otherwise, someone else will take the better traffic lane, get the doctor's appointment, be more skilled in quick grocery shopping, and get the haircut done. We don't have the luxury of slowing down. We're fighting for every millimeter of space; we must be alert and ready to respond if someone dares to take it from us. Don't we deserve those little everyday victories against the whole world? No one taught us; we figured it out on our own. If you fight, you're protected; when you're saved, you're ahead! With these invisible enemies, we have to be ready. Just in case. For every possible scenario.

Everything is questioned and under fire. We don't like how we are served in restaurants, we don't like the overactive youngsters, we don't like our employers and coworkers, and we don't like our workplaces. We're angry about climate change and excruciatingly hot summers. In winter, we complain about the freezing temperatures, and in between all this, we don't want to look old. It's too fast, too soon. We panic, thinking we've lost almost two decades of doing nothing. It's harsh to realize that we could have been more beautiful, both inside and out, knowing what we know now. Time is against us, so we're even angrier than we were fifteen minutes ago. We're angry about everything that happened to us and that didn't.

Twenty-somethings are more innovative, faster, more motivated, powerful, and more fearless. They are anchoring the world, and they have TikTok. We have it, too, but our social media skills differ, like Norton Commander and Windows 11. Maybe we are the last cohort of Norton Commanders?

I found an old photo of me from circa 2004. I have the shortest hair you can imagine in that photo. I've sent it to my girlfriends, saying I need to get the same haircut someday when my scale hopefully shows me minus 10. Someday soon.

I thought I'd do that until this summer, but summer is over. I do not like "Lose weight in 30 Days" or "Prepare your bum for summer" challenges. I'm not even a fan of a reading challenge. There are over 200 books on my Goodreads virtual shelves that I still need to read. What will that haircut bring me? Fulfillment? Happiness? Will I look younger? My teeth will still be yellowish from cigarettes. I don't have the power to freeze time, whether my hair is short or long. I might try a "Make your body perfect" summer challenge next summer. Maybe I should start in winter? I still have plenty of time.

11

WINTER. LOVE. LOSS.

Loss. Sadness. Empty days, living in a haze. Do you remember the last gift you gave me —the facial cream set? I don't want to open it, not yet. Maybe never. Because, childishly, of course, I think it'll symbolize the beginning of living without you. The reality in which you are gone. Strange, but from all the memories of us together, I remember the insignificant ones, and the physical evidence of them, like the green raincoat you bought, and us standing at the entrance of the bookshop in Boston, me telling you about all the books I'd buy if I had a bigger suitcase. That green raincoat is now hanging on the wall in my house.

Remember when we went to the winter resort and I had a terrible case of the flu? More than ten years ago, that winter, I started writing my debut novel. You started writing a little later, but that winter was a turning point for us. It seemed we had finally found what we were most passionate about – writing stories.

I just returned from a family trip to the same place yesterday, and you didn't call me to ask in great detail how we were spending our time. I almost heard your voice. Two winters, eleven years apart. One with you. The first without you.

I hate when they say that life goes on. Maybe it's a ridiculous excuse for us to stay sane. Perhaps it does, accompanied by memories, voices, scents, and constant questioning. What if, what if, what if?!

12

ARE WE THE CHAMPIONS?

"Where have you been all these years?" – My aqua-aerobics instructor asked me while I was trying to focus on stretching my right leg in the water, and her question interrupted me from silently counting alongside her. How am I going to fit nearly ten years of absence and my life since my last session into a five-minute explanation? – I thought. Really, where have I been all this time, and what have I been doing?

I've been writing. I've been working on different jobs from TV content planning to newspaper reporting, I've been procrastinating, I've been traveling, I've been editing, I've been doing nothing, and I've been watching endless hours on TV. That pretty much would sum up my life in five minutes, but I didn't say a word of it, because exercising next to me was a true champion, and no matter what extraordinary story I would tell, hers would always beat mine. Her achievements are incomparably greater. Besides, who cares? Are our lives worth speaking about? How do we measure our success? And why, above all, do we so badly want to be successful and accomplished in the eyes of others?

Five other women of different age groups were in the swimming pool, and all of them seemed perfectly happy and busy with their lives as mothers and grandmothers. I suppose I was the only one constantly blaming myself for never doing enough, living as if there would be another time, another chance, another life where I could erase the mistakes.

"Being humble just doesn't cut it anymore," my friend told me the other day, and probably she's right. But is the swimming pool the right place to tell what you've been up to?

The swimming pool for me is the most vulnerable place, and apart from silently counting in my mind, I can't help but think about what part of my body my swimsuit is properly covering, or else, I'm trying to remember whether I shaved my legs and armpits.

And you have to see my pink hat. My abdomen looks like I've just swallowed two gigantic balloons. I'm always rushing out of the session as if I'm never going to return. While we do squats, I'm a champion of sneaking a glance at the clock, calculating how much time is left until the end. Plus, I'm a champion of scraped nail polish and wet hair, although I'm wearing that stupid pink hat, and I'm the super-mega champion of being jealous of all the women who manage to get out of the swimming pool as if they're just out of the beauty parlor. That, as you probably know by reading this far, is not me. My story is about forgetting flip-flops, towels, and facial and body creams. On a side note, I don't look like a Victoria's Secret model, whether in a swimsuit or not. Squeezing into a swimsuit is a skill, I must admit. "So why do you keep going to aqua aerobics classes, if it seems you pretty much hate all of it?" You might ask.

Because I'm stubborn, and I'm the champion of "despite", and mainly because it can be a good story – I would say. "Everything is copy," –Nora Ephron's mother said.

I love inventing stories.

"Hey, where are you? Dreaming?" My instructor asks me, and I smile in return. She doesn't need to know I'm going to buy a massive piece of chocolate cake on my way home.

13

THIRTY-EIGHT DAYS

Scrolling my Facebook feed this morning, I stumbled upon an eight–year–old Spaniel-Breton ready for adoption. His owner has died. Immediately, I wanted to call you to tell you I'd love to adopt him. We would then discuss that he's not a puppy and that he's probably very sad and lost. We would say what we both know: how time-consuming caring for a senior dog can be. You'd talk me out of adopting him eventually, not because you didn't love dogs, but because you hated sadness and even a slight hint of an unhappy ending.

Of all the things we've talked about over a zillion cups of coffee or glasses of wine, we never talked about death. Our deaths, mine or yours. Never seriously. It always felt like we had everything in front of us. Everything – the cities we wanted to go back to or the new ones we wanted to explore, the books we planned to write, the life we wanted to live, joyously, fully. We wanted to go to Istanbul this summer for either your birthday or mine and stay in the same hotel Agatha Christie frequented. We planned to take a trip on the famous Orient Express someday because we both adored Italy.

We planned, and you always joked that nothing ever went as planned.

I often think, what would you do if I died? Would your sorrow be different? What would your ordinary day be like? How would you cope? And I know you'd be stronger. You'd probably color your hair several times. As idiotic as it is, it makes me smile because I'm more than sure you'd be mad at the stylist, who chose the wrong color, of course.

"Finally, your haircut is perfect, I love it," you told me several months ago when I didn't like mine.

I won't change it, I promise.

It's been thirty-eight days without you.

14

MY NEIGHBOR BENJAMIN

Benjamin is a Bobtail living in an apartment building next to mine —a fluffy, giant of a dog. I saw him just yesterday, playing with his little human at the stadium. The moment I saw them, the image of a little boy running happily with his dog stuck in my mind; I knew I would never forget it.

I remember each second of that little encounter: the green grass of the stadium, the lush green color of the trees, the peacefulness of the summer afternoon —no noise, just a boy and his dog, and his grandma sitting nearby.

I wonder if she's captured that image too. Several minutes, not more, but so profound in its beauty. Why do our minds choose to remember specific images and moments over others? What makes those moments unique? Why are they special to us, personally? I don't have answers to these questions, but I vividly remember an autumn walk in the park with my dog years ago.

As a dog owner for almost twelve years, I've been walking in the park nearly every day, but there are just glimpses of our walks that I remember. The crispiness of early mornings, the sound of leaves under my feet, the trees changing colors, the smell of the final days of autumn, and the beginning of winter in the air.

I miss those walks, those days, those moments, that laughter and joy, chasing after my boisterous dog, playing hide-and-seek, that tranquility of just the two of us, our bond, our stories. I want to feel that again, to be there again, to live in it again, and somehow I know that many years from now, I will remember those moments as the happiest of my life. I can't find another word than beautiful for its mundanity and routine, but trust me on this: life with a dog is a great many things, and above all, it is unforgettable.

I can certainly remember myself as happier at different times, from childhood through adolescence, but when I look back, that single memory of walking with my dog in the park comes to mind. Autumn and Winter. Snowy dog ears, cold black nose, wet paws, wet fur. Us and nature. An ordinary day. A happy day. I'm missing it now. Why can't we understand it when it is happening? Why can't we know right then that this will be one of the happiest times? Why do we think happiness means something huge?

Do we idealize our past and are attached to it just because it's gone? Do we fear it won't happen with the same intensity anymore? Do we believe our past, which we often revisit, is better than what's ahead? Are we eager to romanticize it? Why do I try to revive past emotions, feelings, and memories? Maybe my subconscious is trying to tell me, "Yes, you will be happy many more times, but first, let's get you a dog?"

15

THE POOL

Eight of us were seated by the pool on a hot July Saturday. I hid from the excruciating heat in the tree's shadow, having all I wanted near me –half a pack of cigarettes and freshly brewed coffee. Some of my girlfriends were lounging, while others laughed, splashed water, took pictures of us, and even sang along to the popular Italian tune chosen as the soundtrack for the lazy weekend outside the town. That summer, we turned forty-nine. In a year, we are turning fifty, I thought, while explaining why I didn't want to sunbathe or swim in the turquoise water of the brand-new pool my friend just added to her beautiful house hidden on the hill with old pine trees. It felt as if we were on a vacation in Italy, just fifteen minutes outside Tbilisi, grabbing the opportunity to recharge and shut our minds off for a little while.

We are all childhood and university friends. We have known each other long enough to avoid engaging in polite small talk and just be silent. Yet, something nudged me.

A feeling of discontent and light sadness. I looked at my friends and myself, our faces still young, our bodies holding histories of childbirth, miscarriages, exercise, diets, and overeating, of self-love and self-destroying, of battling with aging and surrender, of childhood scars and beauty experiments, of lost chances and heartbreaks, of longing for new beginnings, rewriting our failures. And beneath the surface, what saddened me even more was how estranged I felt. We were seated just a few meters apart, but it felt like a lifetime. I wondered how much we still knew about each other —our worries, our joys, our secrets, and our unfulfilled wishes. As we sat there, around the pool, I saw it as a metaphor for us. Together, yet apart. Knowing every gesture of each other by heart, yet not knowing anything at all about ourselves and who we have become.

We've all changed so much since our childhood and college years. It seems that somewhere between marriages and divorces, new jobs and old crushes, grown-up children and self-discoveries, extensive travels, losses, grief, successes, and setbacks, extraverts transforming into introverts, fashion and movie aficionados transforming into la dolce vita connoisseurs and la dolce vita connoisseurs transforming into politically savvy forty-somethings, somewhere in the whirlwind of our multi-dimensional lives and our shared memories we lost our deep friendship. Or perhaps it has evolved into something entirely different: a calmer bond that requires no justification, no approval, and no day-to-day communication. Maybe we became more private and reserved? Perhaps we've learned to treasure our time and our private space?

Maybe we no longer need each other's advice on tackling small and big crises in our lives, nor do we need to share our personal experiences immediately.

A friend of mine just remarked that she only needs a glass of cold Champagne and lying by the pool to be happy. That's her know-how of forgetting a demanding job, and a series of relationships that could have brought more joy. So what if she's right and that's all that matters? A bubbly cold glass of Champagne and a turquoise pool, for starters?

16

ALMOST DUST

I did an online Adult Autism test yesterday; that said, I have fifteen percent of autism in me. No surprise! Deep down, I knew I had some autistic traits, maybe. There's no need to take an online test to learn that I'm not the easiest person to be around. I can be funny, joyous, and sarcastic, and make you laugh till you pee, but when I'm alone, I'm sad.

I'm getting older, and my friends and family members are getting older, sadder, or maybe wiser? We're so centered on our own lives, worries, and problems—squeezing it all into messages, simplifying our feelings—and it all seems easy and passable, like a five-minute life update. We all live in that five-minute update cycle. No one has lengthy conversations anymore —or is it just me and my bubble? We're okay with sharing and knowing tidbits of our lives, and it's enough. We don't have time to delve deeper into each other's problems, stories, or lives. Five minutes on the phone or chatting online is enough. The truth is that no one wants to know what we feel and what we're going through in detail—even our closest friends. Or, we don't want to burden them with irrelevant news from our lives. We're used to dealing with our little demons on our own. We must be strong, successful, motivated, inspired, independent, and optimistic —the "I can handle everything" queens and overachievers. Yet, somewhere along the way to becoming better, more beautiful, and more successful, we lose ourselves. I miss the time we spent in cafes talking, smoking cigarettes, and drinking our coffee or glasses of wine for hours. We don't have time for lengthy soul stripteases anymore, and the worst part is that no one seems to mind. We're so obsessed with moving forward; we're so eager to forget our pains and just run toward the so-called future that we're sure has to be better and brighter. We so deeply want to erase all our traumas – sometimes it seems we forget who we are.

It's so firmly ingrained in us that we must be the best versions of ourselves; we constantly strive to reinvent our identity, encompassing physical, spiritual, and mental aspects. We're good, but something's always missing, just a tiny detail that will make us flawless. A Botox, maybe? A super-tanned body? Intermittent fasting? Excruciating exercise?

What if I don't want to be better, wiser, or more beautiful? What if I want to be just whoever I am? Maybe I want to be a nobody—Jane Doe. Perhaps I want to be enough without needing a cliché positive quote. Why do I have to adjust, be flexible, and be social? Why can't I just be? Whomever I am. The minuscule piece of the universe. Almost dust.

17

I WANT TO…

I want to scream your name so that you can hear me wherever you are and return. I want to go back in time and live every moment with you again. I want to change your story. Our story. I want to see you old, us, old. A month ago in Paris, as I wandered through the streets, I found myself constantly searching for older women who were charming, beautiful, and stylish. I imagined you at their age, wondering how you would look, what you would wear, and where you would travel. How many books would you have written? I will never know all of that; I can only imagine, and it breaks my heart.

Denial, anger, bargaining, depression, and acceptance. Yes, I just Googled the five stages of grief, and immediately I knew you'd laugh at my silly habit of Googling everything. I Googled Lampedusa this morning, and from what I've read and seen, it seems stunning, much like the entire island of Sicily. But rather than going to Sicily, I would travel somewhere very far away. Alaska, winter, dog-sledding, and Jack London influences come to mind, and I know you'd laugh again because, as much as I love winter, being alone in Alaska sounds too extreme. Visiting a ranch somewhere in Montana, perhaps John Dutton's Yellowstone? I think I'm falling for Kevin Costner again. And I want to talk to you about how good he is in that show. I'm remembering the giant poster our mutual friend had in her bedroom from one of his much earlier movies, and how we both wanted to steal it from her.

I want to run, hide, disappear, vanish. I wonder what stage of grief that is? What stage of grief makes you almost burst in envy, witnessing lifelong friendships around you and wondering why you've been ripped off that possibility?

I would love to know what you think of AI and of my AI-narrated audiobooks. Do you like the voices I've chosen? Or would you say you prefer reading them rather than listening to them? AI is everywhere since you're gone, even in my nerve-wracking language app, and it's a massive debate on AI and intellectual property, and all the hazards it implies. Yes, I'm re-learning French, and today's lesson started with a phrase, "Je mange trop de biscuit." What a coincidence—I am eating a lot of biscuits, ice cream, and chocolate, then coffee—but I'm assuring myself that I want to get slim and wear bikinis, either in Montana, Alaska, or Sicily.

Remember our white jeans and striped sandals project after you lost weight, when you said you needed a tiny bit more before you'd buy them for summer? I wrote about myself fantasizing about white jeans, but deep inside, I know that without you by my side, I don't care.

I want to write a new book of essays, but what's the point if you're never going to read it? Entering my kitchen with a bottle of champagne, beaming, happy, ready to celebrate?

I WANT TO…

I want to… scream.

I want to remember us seated in a buzzing Istanbul café on a rainy day as you ask the waiter, "Do you know what I want?" A simple, straightforward question – a direct translation from Georgian to English, maybe too direct, bare, with no polite chit-chat. It sounded funny, and we teased you a lot afterward. You knew what we wanted to taste from the vast choice of exceptional Turkish mezes, fish, and seafood. You knew Istanbul and its hidden gems better than anyone, and we followed you without much thinking, safely, in awe of what beautiful part of the city we would discover next. Every trip with you from Istanbul to Paris was a discovery, as we delved into its tastes, arts, streets, shops, and museums. You were the best travel companion one could think of.

Do you know what I want?

I want to call you and tell you about the mesmerizing colors of the sea in Crete. I want to tell you that out of ten days, I spent four lying in bed with a fever, and I want to hear you laugh.

I want to tell you I'm considering going to Rome alone. I know you'd say to me it's the best idea you've heard from me lately.

I want to discuss the book you're writing and let you know that I have no idea what my next book will be about. I want to hear you say with certainty that it would probably be a novel, just as you told me several years ago that I would write a collection of short stories, and in several months, You Will Have a Black Labrador was written. I love it the most because you're there too.

I want you to call me and tell me you're popping by and urgently need a coffee, and we'd sit on my balcony and drink coffee and talk. About what? About everything and nothing, as you would say.

Both you and I loved September. We both felt that it always meant a beginning and were eager to return from our holidays, meet and chat, exhale, inhale, and prepare for the rest of the year.

I want to tell you that in the months since you left, it feels tasteless, colorless, and joyless. I want to tell you that I'm watching Chef's Table and wonder why seeing someone preparing food brings so much comfort. Remember, we ate the best pumpkin ravioli in a tiny restaurant next to our hotel in Paris, exhausted, our feet burning from running around the city, and wanting to see as much as we could. Remember how I didn't want you to pay for our stay, and we laughed about it? The young girl at the reception asked whether the Georgian word "Ara" meant "no," and we replied that it did. A title for a short essay was born right there.

Everything has changed. It's a strange September. You are gone. I'm afraid to forget.

18

WHITE JEANS

I've never been skinny. I've never been 'chubby'. I've always been somewhere in between. I swung from normal to slightly above my usual weight of 60+ kg during my twenties, thirties, and early forties, when I suddenly transformed into a woman who wore loose dresses and baggy jeans. Loose dresses? I can count them to two. The rest of my wardrobe is a mixture of oversized shirts and pants. I do have a dress I still would love to wear —a light brown summer dress, almost identical to the one Julia Roberts wears in Pretty Woman —at the Polo match, remember? But I wore it exactly once at my friend's wedding, and it's been hanging around ever since. Honestly, I don't want to find it and look at it. And what's the point of writing about it?

That's not what I'd like to write about. I want to write about white jeans — not too slim or skinny, and not too baggy either. Not the boyfriend cut, no, the regular fit, that I'd wear with a tank top. I'm getting obsessed with them. I eye-shop and pretend I'm wearing them, but I never buy, because I would need to lose a certain amount of weight to fit into the white jeans I'm fantasizing about. I have to weigh in at minus twenty kilograms, precisely. So, where is the conflict in the story? What's the obstacle preventing the character (that said, me) from getting what she wants? Her (my) laziness? Her (my) inability or unwillingness to diet? Her (my) lack of motivation? If I do lose the weight, will it make me happier? I doubt. Theoretically, I would love to have a slimmer, tanner, and more fit body, like the young, beautiful women in my Pilates class. Oh, I'm great at theory, but the real me is too far from it. The real me is still afraid of buying white jeans, not just in a hypothetical future. The real me wants those white jeans to be a mirage, an illusion.

As I'm writing this, I'm wearing a T-shirt with "Everything I see I owe to Spaghetti," written in red and black. I love it. I often wear it to my Pilates and Yoga.

19

LITTLE BLACK LAPTOP

We don't thank objects, do we? I know it might sound a little weird. Last week, I was searching for an essay I had written years ago. I had to turn on my old black HP Mini to see if it was buried among the documents, photos, and old emails. I didn't find it, but I found myself from around 2009 to 2019. The whole decade of my life was there: old TV guides – from when I worked at the TV station, photos of me and my dog in the park. That winter, I quit one of my jobs and started writing what would later become my first novel.

Folders with manuscripts edited, unedited, reedited, emails to editor, editor's notes, book covers I had to choose from, galleys, letters to my friends who were reading every single chapter as I wrote, snapshots from Facebook in a pre–messenger era, with "WHERE THE HELL ARE YOU?!" always written in all caps on our Facebook walls, a code to something urgent happening.

Photos from a trip to Istanbul, then from a trip to New York, another draft of a new book I started writing, and didn't finish. A folder of unfinished drafts labeled 'Lavignia'. She had to be one of the main characters, but I've never written her story.

Beginnings without endings.... Jobs applied for and never got.

I didn't expect it to turn into a time-traveling device, where I could meet myself in a life that now feels distant. A portal to the past, a time capsule holding everything: our friendships, happy days, secrets, and changes... No nostalgia, just a look back at who we were then and what worried us. Rejections, transitions, transformations. Ten years ago, we were at the beginning of our lives as we are now. Ready to change and start something different, scary, and unknown, becoming who we are now. That laptop is a witness to all of that.

My little black laptop barely works now; it took me at least fifteen minutes to get online with it. Those fifteen minutes felt like hours, and I grew angry and impatient. I was ready to shut it down, but then I realized I had never said thank you to it. I forgot how grateful I was for keeping everything I wrote—those ridiculously awful drafts, the memories, the letters to friends, the chats, the silly messages. So, consider this a belated thank-you note to the black HP Mini, also known as the butterfly, as we affectionately called it.

"Put the kettle on, I'm gonna pop in for a minute." My friend called me one December, before Christmas, years ago, and showed up at my doorstep, holding a bag with a new laptop. "The butterfly has to rest now. I can't see you struggling with that little one any longer," she added, referring to my old laptop. She was right. Batteries were changed, and new adapters were purchased, but the "butterfly" was getting slower each day, so I placed it on a shelf in the study to rest. We both sensed it was time for a new story.

20

STILL ME?

I'm terrified of losing my memory, and that's one of the fears that consumes me. Yesterday, I couldn't find my black pants. Gone. Vanished. Disappeared. My grandmother's sister had a strange case of dementia; she was fixated on time. Every day, she would call and ask what time it was. She remembered our phone numbers by heart and knew who she was calling, but she couldn't recall the time. She would keep asking and checking throughout the day, much to my father's dismay, who thought she was playing a prank on him.

I used to have a great memory. Better than most of my friends, I could recount episodes from our school or university years that no one else remembered, down to the insignificant details of outfits we wore on any given day.

I never forgot anniversaries or other important dates. I used to be the one who would know. Not anymore. Twice, I caught myself re-watching the TV shows I've already seen, realizing it by their end credits. What about personal milestones? I'm ashamed to say that I don't remember the exact dates or months when my books were published, unless a Facebook memory pops up or I check my author dashboard. Well, I still remember the emotions I felt, ripping off the parcels with copies of books inside, but I can't recall the exact dates. Seasons? Gone.

Yesterday, I had a mild panic attack when my black pants vanished into the abyss of the closet. After an hour of frantic search, they finally reappeared, next to my old raincoat. If I were into writing a horror fantasy, I would make my closet the main villain, with a scary grin appearing on its surface whenever I'm about to retrieve something from it. "Nice try. Keep looking. Oops, your time's up." It would tease me, reminding me of a hidden object game I used to play, where I never found what I was searching for and never reached the end.

What scares me is the prospect of not remembering people, places, and events. Who we are without the memories that shaped us?

I don't know which Netflix algorithm decided to suggest that I watch "Still Alice" yesterday. Coincidence?

I love that movie and the book. I've read it twice and watched the film numerous times. That, at least, I remember for now.

21

THERE WAS A GARDEN ONCE

"Nin, you overslept again? We're here and waiting." Lena's voice on the phone awakens me. I put my phone on the nightstand and run into the bathroom. In ten minutes, I'm ready. "Where are you going? We walked already," Mom tells me as I grab the leash. "They're waiting for me in the park," I reply and run down the stairs with Figu, my ten-year-old English Cocker Spaniel. It's June, and by afternoon, it'll be hot and humid already. I don't want to miss a day of walking in the park.

Figu's old, and it's the only joy left for him to run hectically, eat the grass and everything disgusting from a rotten rat to a half-rotten squirrel, or roll in excrement. Lena is on her third walk when we finally meet. I let my dog off-leash and stay with Lena and her Boston Terrier, Chip, who, like Figu, is old and trembles a little. Chip arrived from the US, a gift from Lena's daughter.

We are joined by Tina and her Irish terrier, Billy. His amber eyes are clever and thoughtful, his expression alert and a little surprised whenever I search for Figu in a high-pitched voice that echoes over the park. Breathless, I run and call him, finally find the troublemaker, return to Tina and Lena, and ask what exactly we were talking about.

"Khaled Hosseini. The Kite Runner, what a book, thanks for recommending it," Tina says, and we continue walking, while Lena tells us about the new TV shows she just watched and promises to read Hosseini's work.

Figu never gives a damn about our intellectual ramblings. He has a mission of chasing a fat yellow Labrador, which he happens to be in love with. By the end of our morning walk, I'm usually exhausted.

All winter, spring, and half of the summer that year, I spent talking about books, films, TV shows, travels, yoga, religion, kids, husbands, love, and sometimes politics, and always about dogs. Tina recounts her latest trip to Northern France, specifically to Deauville and Trouville, and the beautiful white horses she saw on the beach. "It's my happy place," she says dreamily. Our group expands. We are joined by Manana, who tells us about medieval Georgian literature, but I particularly love the antics of her cocker spaniel, Pepe, and her puppies. Irina, also a member of our group, suggests celebrating something, and we agree, gulping vodka shots in the mornings that winter. Lena is planning her trip to the US, and I am writing a book, which I keep secret.

"Did you know there was a garden once, before the park?" Lena asks me as we walk another round. I didn't know about the garden, but I remember when this park opened. I tried to spend every weekend there with my closest friend, Keta, when we were at school. As soon as the weekend arrived, I called our driver, Marlen, picked up Keta, and off we went to the park to check out the carousels. The main catch was to steal her from the boring piano lessons she had on Saturdays. Playing Maykapar etudes, we thought, would never be as exciting as spending a day in the park. I must say, Keta was much more talented and advanced at playing the piano than I was. I skipped my lessons all the time, and after not showing up for two consecutive months, my music teacher finally called and asked what was going on. A massive scandal followed. My father wanted me to be a pianist, or at least play well, but I hated it.

The park was the only place we were allowed to go on our own. One winter, we stayed at the carousels for more than an hour, froze our butts off, and developed an idiosyncrasy towards any swings, roller coasters, and attractions.

I have numerous photos taken in the park, all of which are at the entrance, in front of the Pierrot statue. There we are — my cousin and I, in similar coats. Red and brown. I'm wearing an awful white scarf with little white dots and some dark blue stockings. We seem happy. I also have photos of me and Keta, aged nine or ten, at the same place—the Pierrot statue again. It's summer, and music lessons and school are over. We're wearing matching pants and matching sneakers. Her hair is green and messy. In two years, I'll have a poodle, Charlie, and we'll be spending even more time at the park.

My brother wasn't thrilled to have a poodle. He wanted a Cocker Spaniel, but I was just as stubborn. I threw a tantrum in front of the poodle puppy owner and my embarrassed mom. For the next two years, every photo I took, Charlie was there. He died two years later. We were at our summer house when Mom called and told us it was over. I cried, my cousin cried. My brother seemed devastated, too. I stopped going to the park.

It was the last year of school when I decided I wanted to have a dog again. My brother was going to study in the US, and he didn't care whether it was a dog or an elephant.

Jerry, a black English cocker spaniel, ate all our house plants and some of my father's socks and jackets. We blamed Jerry for licking drops from my father's Metaxa bottle, which proudly stood in our dining room, waiting for my dad's friends to taste it, but we stole a glass a day and almost emptied it before they had a chance.

Mom called when we were at the winter resort of Bakuriani, saying that Jerry died from the dog-fight wounds.

For the next fifteen years, I didn't have a dog, nor did I go to the park. The park in the nineties was dim and scary. It needed a certain amount of heroism to walk there, and I was never a hero.

My ovarian cyst made me decide to get a dog for the third time. Whether it was something Freudian, a sublimation, or an obsession, I never searched so hard for the right puppy and found a blue roan one in Moscow. "Why are you getting a dog from Moscow? Can't you get it here, in Tbilisi?" I was asked again and again. "I just need that exact puppy in a blue roan color", I would shut the conversation down. In December of 2006, Figu arrived in a crate at Tbilisi airport, and it felt euphoric. "You should have studied animal psychology instead of film," my father often remarked, and neither of us liked the joke, but we laughed nevertheless, thinking about the choices we made. Figu never found our existential dialogues worth listening to; he was fascinated by stealing handkerchiefs from my father's pockets whenever he got the chance.

"Do you think he sensed anything?" Mom asked when my father passed away, referring to Figu. I doubt. I don't remember. I remember our crowded house, sending Figu away for a week to our dog-walker, and bringing him back after the funeral, with his voice completely gone from all the excessive barking.

I transformed into a crazy dog person. I skipped work for vet appointments, calling my boss to tell him I had a dog emergency. I changed several jobs in between, quit working, then found a new one, and the only constant was our walks in the park, regardless of the season.

"Don't be late tomorrow," Lena told me, and we hugged each other. In a couple of weeks, she was leaving, but I didn't want us to feel sad about it. "See you tomorrow at 8:30 as usual," I said, and she walked me to the corner of my street.

Very late that night, I heard a strange sound, like a roar, a thunder. It was raining heavily, but I went back to sleep.

"Do not go anywhere near the park, it's flooded, it's gone, and animals from the Zoo are in the streets," – My brother called me first thing in the morning. I ran to the balcony. The park was covered in muddy water. As we later discovered, people died. The Zoo adjacent to the park was destroyed. Animals were dead.

I took pictures from my balcony and sent them to Tina. She cried. I've been to the park merely twice after the flood. Although the park had been renovated, we didn't visit it much. Then Chip died, and then Pepe, Figu, and Billy. Lena lives in the US now. Tina lives in another district near the old Hippodrome. I still need to check with Lena to see if she has had a chance to read The Kite Runner.

22

INSTEAD OF A PROLOGUE & AN EPILOGUE

"*Instead*" is a great word. What a genius discovery! I keep doing a lot of things instead of what I should be doing: editing my manuscript. An unfinished, nearly finished, or far from finished, and I have three different versions of it. I forget which one is edited and start reediting what I think is already polished to a readable level every morning, until I get a notification from one of the shopping sites offering to buy a Christmas-themed couch cover.

The shopping site tells me I'll get a considerable discount if I buy 10 items. I've already purchased slippers, earplugs, a magnifying mirror, socks, and another pair of slippers in a different color—grey instead of beige. I looked into the magnifying mirror only once, and my migraine started. There's no need to look at my face, magnified seventy times. What I know now is that I need new tweezers and a new moisturizer, possibly from a Korean brand that keeps appearing in my Instagram feed, promising to restore a much-needed glow to my skin and boost my overall confidence.

I've also bought chair protectors – wrong size. When I was little, we had floor polish and felt chair protectors, and I used them to "skate" from our living room to our kitchen, and back, pretending I was a figure skater. I imagined standing at the "Kiss and Cry" and later hearing "6:0, 6:0, 6:0" from the judges. I became a film critic and a writer instead, and figure skating now uses a new judging system.

But let's get back to that magic word - instead. Instead of making revisions, cutting unnecessary parts, and rereading or thinking about a blurb, I'm searching stock photos for cover inspiration. What is my unfinished book going to be about? My book will be a memoir in essays—creative nonfiction/narrative nonfiction, however you'd like to define it.

Why am I typing dog park?! That book is not intended to be about dogs. It's about many things, but certainly not about dogs. It's about grief, and memory, and loss, and longing, and love, and life in general, but I don't really like the phrase –life in general, because, honestly, what does it mean? Doesn't it sound vague and pretentious? I need to come up with a better phrase to sum it up, but nothing comes to mind at the moment. What kind of writer am I?! I don't even have a title yet. It seems all the great titles are already taken. I am jealous. Very jealous. I envy every great title that exists, like Bonjour Tristesse or One Hundred Years of Solitude, and even The Idiot.

That said, I dismiss the idea of the dog park on my soon-to-be-finished book cover. I'd rather put a couch on it, or a woman sipping a coffee, holding a magnifying glass. A sofa with a Christmassy blanket, which I'm afraid I'll have to buy.

An idea, an impulse, a thought, an observation, even a dream, can make you start to write, but how do you know when to stop? When does the story have to come to an end? If you're writing fiction, it might be slightly easier when the plot reaches its culmination and climax, say, you're writing a 'who-done-it' thriller, the villain is caught, the case is solved, or if it's a romance novel, the enemies become lovers, lovers may become spouses, all of them getting a big, fat happy –end, but if you're writing nonfiction essays? How to know when to stop?

Even if I were a reincarnation of Mark Twain—which, too obviously, I am not—I doubt anyone outside my family would read a five-hundred-page-long personal story, no matter how insightful, witty, funny, or heart-wrenching it is. You don't have to write another piece about your beloved dog, or cat, or a hamster, your childhood traumas, or your favorite Crème Brûlée.

Ending a story (a book) can be sad, liberating, exhausting, and joyful all at once, but how do you know that you've written everything you intended to?

Is it a feeling? A hunch? Does it depend on craft and mastery?

I don't have the answer; I'm still figuring it out. I'm reading the manuscript, rearranging the sequence of stories, cutting parts out, reading, rewriting, swinging between doubt and more doubt, and preparing for the next phase: editing—the phase I love. Then I hate it, and then I hate whatever I've written. After that, I love again, until finally it's ready, and the world pauses for a second before I hit publish.

23

YOU KNOW NOTHING

Ten years ago, in September 2015, I published my first book, followed by three more in 2019, 2020, and 2021. I'm no longer a debut author. The excitement of my first book being published has worn off, and I recognize these feelings well. The pre-publication cheer, the joy of seeing your book in print, the exhaustion afterward, the initial spark of thinking about writing a new one—writing, editing, publishing, marketing, reaching out to bloggers, social media promotion, selling, not selling, writing again, procrastinating, editing, preparing for publishing, publishing, selling, not selling, writing, editing, polishing, publishing…

Is it the writing journey I imagined? To be very honest? No. As much as I'm happy with choosing the self-publishing route, it certainly can be nerve-wracking, especially when you have to make decisions entirely on your own, from selecting the right editor to creating your book cover or learning how to format your manuscript, and no one tells you that it's a never-ending learning curve. Marketing and ads, social media promotions, blogging, blurbs, synopsis, and figuring out how to pitch your

450-page book in three words.

"You know nothing, Jon Snow." Well, exactly. First, you're overwhelmed by how much you have to learn, and later, you're flabbergasted by all the information on publishing you receive.

Many times, too many times, it may seem that the whole voyage is about failing and failing some more, but then the "despite" comes, and somewhere along the way, you realize it's the "despite" that keeps you moving forward.

It took me a decade to become calmer. Calmer about writing badly. Calmer about receiving both positive and negative feedback, calmer about days, weeks, months spent not writing, calmer about book sales, calmer about unfinished writing projects, calmer about letting go. I don't regret. I accept. I expect. I'm more interested in what's in there next. A new book? One? Two, or three? Writing, editing, polishing, publishing, writing….

24

HOW TO END A BOOK?

Nothing original here; every story has a conclusion. I've been thinking about how to wrap up the imaginary book—what should the final essay be? Hopeful? Humorous? Thought-provoking? Sad? Nostalgic? Then, out of nowhere, my mother decides we need to renovate the kitchen. This results in a complete invasion of my privacy by two painters working nonstop and our lovely housekeeper, who keeps me company by showing me beautiful images of her village—the roses, her garden, and the ancient church seen from her yard. I'm egoistically picturing myself in the same setting, surrounded by forests, meadows, and dahlias. I see myself walking in the woods with my dog(s), coming home to a freshly made salad, warm Georgian bread, and tomatoes bought at the local market. I know what my house looks like. It's a wooden, two-bedroom cottage. I've written enough about my dream house and dogs, so there's no need to include them in the final essay. However, I worry I'm obsessed with idyllic villages, and my Pinterest is full of barns, shaggy houses, and cottages in all four seasons.

"Your next obsession awaits" – that's the notification from Pinterest I just got. My new obsession turns out to be coffee and Autumn leaves, but I ignore them for now.

"Are you really writing? Am I disturbing you?" The question brings me back into the reality of my living room. Our housekeeper kindly asks, and I smile, mentally noting to buy gigantic, noise-reducing headphones for the next time I'll be writing the last chapter of my book. I'm distracted. The grand finale just flew out of the window in the October sky. Is this the best sentence I could come up with? But it is October! At least I'm season accurate.

I start writing again, after a third cup of coffee and a fifth cigarette. My phone rings. It's mom. "How are they doing?" She asks. "Don't forget to tell them that the kitchen door has to be slightly beige, not white."

It appears that the kitchen door is already painted white, much to her dismay.

Out of nowhere, I suddenly remember that years ago, my editor asked me why the protagonist of my debut novel at the time was still living with her mother in her mid-thirties. What does she mean by why? There's no why. There's just the reality. That's our culture. Our tradition of generations of families living under one roof, dear editor. I'm fifty-one, and it's just the two of us: my mom and me living together.

I reenter the living room to keep writing and have a quick cigarette. Nothing comes to mind.

This kitchen renovation is killing my creativity. I could go to my bedroom and work from there, but the Wi-Fi is nonexistent in that part of the house, and even though I can write, I can't check Instagram during my writing breaks, every ten minutes.

From the living room, I hear the noise. Two men are painting the walls. Our kitchen is now white instead of beige. I'm trying to focus, but my mind drifts back to the memory. The kitchen table is flooded with Georgian food. It's the New Year. Guests — our family friends — are arriving. My mother is running back and forth from the kitchen to the living room to serve the dishes. The living room is filled with a mix of smells: perfume, cigarettes, and alcohol; toast, laughter, and singing; and the sounds of piano and guitar. My sole function is to answer the apartment door and greet the guests. Then, when everyone's gone and the dinner is over, I help my mom clean the table.

Our kitchen, like any other, is the heart of our lives. It's for our closest ones, for the hidden and personal, private stories that are told while we're seated close to each other, facing one another, talking, laughing, discussing, gossiping, planning...

Another memory comes right after the first one. It's early morning, and we are all gathered in the kitchen, having breakfast. My mom, dad, and my brother are there. Our parents are rushing to work, but we'd love to stay home and skip school. The New Year festivities are over, and we're back to everyday life...

The third memory is of you, bringing coffee capsules, roasted sunflower seeds, and waffles. Why waffles? I'm not sure, but they're delicious with coffee. We talk. We laugh. We gossip. We plan. We have no idea what's coming our way....

Much of our lives, especially during the pandemic, centered on this 12-square-meter space. We didn't want to sit in any other room; somehow, the kitchen became our shield, comfort, a world within a world—a safer place. It was the kitchen and the balcony, where pigeons had nested the previous year, two weeks before Easter. I used to hate pigeons. I am still not fond of birds, but I have become tolerant of the ones that chose our balcony as their temporary home. The little ones were growing too fast. The whole family of four flew away. We haven't had a new nest or a new pigeon family this year, but sometimes I see the grey-white pigeon sitting on a flower pot, and I want to believe it's the same one that flew away. I hope it returned.

About the Author

Nino Gugunishvili is the author of the women's fiction novel Friday Evening, Eight O'clock (2015) and two essay collections: You Will Have a Black Labrador, published in 2019, and From My Balcony to Yours, published in 2020. She lives in Tbilisi, Georgia.

Printed in Dunstable, United Kingdom